Church Year

Series B
Pentecost I

Study Guide

By John Juedes

CPH
SAINT LOUIS

Edited by Thomas J. Doyle

Write to the Library for the Blind, 1333 S. Kirkwood Road, St. Louis, MO 63122-7295 to obtain this study in braille or in large print for the visually impaired.

3558 S. Jefferson Avenue, St. Louis, MO 63118-3968
Manufactured in the United States of America

1 2 3 4 5 6 7 8 9 10 05 04 03 02 01 00 99 98 97 96

Contents

Introduction

About the Series

This course is 1 of 12 in the Church Year series. The Bible studies in this series are tied to the 3-year lectionary. These studies give participants the opportunity to explore the Old Testament lesson (or lesson from the book of Acts during the Easter season), the Epistle lesson, and the Gospel lesson appointed for each Sunday of the church year. Also, optional studies give participants the opportunity to study in-depth the lessons appointed for festivals that fall on days other than Sunday (e.g., Ascension, Reformation, Christmas, Christmas Eve, Maundy Thursday, Good Friday, Epiphany).

Book 1 for years A, B, and C in the lectionary series will include 17 studies for the Scripture lessons appointed for the Sundays and festival days in Advent, Christmas, and Epiphany. Book 2 will include 17 studies for the lessons appointed for the Sundays and festival days in Lent and Easter and of lessons appointed for Ascension and Pentecost. Book 3 (15 sessions) and 4 (15 sessions) for years A, B, and C will include studies that focus on the lessons appointed for the Pentecost season.

After a brief review and study of the Scripture lessons appointed for a Sunday or festival day, each study is designed to help participants draw conclusions about each of the lessons, compare the lessons, discover a unifying theme in the lessons (if possible), and apply the theme to their lives. At the end of each study, the Scripture lessons for the next Sunday and/or festival day are assigned in preparation for the next study. The Leaders Guide for each course provides additional information on appointed lessons, answers to the questions in the Study Guide, a suggested process for teaching the study, and devotional or worship activities tied to the theme.

May the Holy Spirit richly bless you as you study God's Word!

Session 1

The Holy Trinity

Deuteronomy 6:4–9; Romans 8:14–17; John 3:1–17

Focus

Theme: *Love the Lord and Serve Him Only!*

Law/Gospel Focus

From conception, we had sinful natures that made us dead in sin and enemies of God. But He miraculously through faith in His Son's death on the cross and resurrection from the dead causes us to be reborn as children of God, transforming our relationship with God from one of fear to one of love.

Objectives

By the power of the Holy Spirit working through God's Word we will

1. revere only one God, rejecting all else that claims to be god or attracts our reverence;
2. love God with all our hearts and express it in concrete ways;
3. find comfort in the assurance that God loves us and forgives us through Christ and seeks to do good for us always.

Opening Worship

Pray together this litany adapted from Psalm 96.

Leader: Sing to the Lord, praise His name;
Participants: For great is the Lord and most worthy of praise.
Leader: Splendor and majesty are before Him;
Participants: Ascribe to the Lord the glory due His name.
Leader: Worship the Lord in the splendor of His holiness;
Participants: Say among the nations, "The Lord reigns!"
Leader: Let everything sing before the Lord;
Participants: for He will judge the world in righteousness and truth.

Introduction

How do people relate to you? If you are an employer, your workers may relate to you as a strict boss. A store clerk may see you as a demanding customer, while a longtime acquaintance may feel you're a good friend. Your spouse may care for you as a husband or wife, while your children love you as their father or mother. No matter who you are, different people relate to you in different ways.

This is also true of God. Different people relate to Him in different ways. How do you relate to God? Do you see God primarily as a

- stringent Judge?
- ever-watchful Policeman?
- strict Boss?
- distant Uncle?
- caring Husband?
- loving Father?

How you see God has many ramifications, because it influences how you pray, worship, trust, obey, witness, and respond to God on many fronts.

1. If a national poll asked Americans how they related to God, which of the images mentioned above (Judge, Policeman, etc.) do you think would receive the most responses? Why? Which ones would perhaps receive the fewest responses? Why?

2. When something bad happens to you, do you feel that God sent it to punish you? or do you think that He is watching you critically to see if you will behave properly under stress? or do you pray for help immediately, sure that God will come to your rescue right away? What does a person's response tell you about the way he or she relates to God?

Through faith strengthened by Word and Sacrament God enables His followers to see Him as a loving Father who responds to them in love.

Inform

Scan these summaries of the Scripture lessons for Holy Trinity, the First Sunday of Pentecost.

Deuteronomy 6:4–9—Ancient Jews considered these verses the great *Shema,* a statement of faith in the one and only true God and of their duty to obey God's commands. Above all, God calls His people to love Him.

Romans 8:14–17—Christians have a unique status as sons and daughters, not slaves, of God. God's Spirit assures us of our high standing—heirs—with God and leads us to follow Him.

John 3:1–17—Nicodemus knew of the duty to obey God's laws, but he did not know of God's love and grace, which are reflected in Christ's sacrifice on the cross and in the Spirit's ability to give us new spiritual life.

These readings focus on how our relationship with God can be one of love rather than one of fear, apathy, or ignorance.

1. Religious Jews carried out the command of Deuteronomy 6:8 literally by making small leather boxes called *phylacteries* in which they placed small written copies of Deuteronomy 6:4–5. They then tied these boxes to their foreheads and hands. Jesus criticized them because they missed the central point of this passage. What important attitude should they have focused on instead? (See Matthew 23:3, 5, 11, 23, 25 for additional attitudes they needed to develop.)

2. The readings for Trinity Sunday highlight the truth that God is three persons in one being—Triune. What words of Deuteronomy 6 emphasize the one-ness of God?

3. How does Romans 8 highlight the Trinity? What does it say about the Father? about the Son? about the Holy Spirit? In what way does the Holy Spirit carry on Christ's work of freeing us from sin? What kind of relationship with God does the Holy Spirit "testify" to?

4. How is the Father, Son, and Holy Spirit each pictured in John 3? What is the work of the Holy Spirit (3:6–7)? the work of the Son for us (3:14, 17)? the work of the Father (3:16)? What common goal does God's work accomplish (3:16)? What does this suggest about the oneness of God?

5. Jesus says that people must be "born again" or "born of the Spirit" to see God's kingdom. What does it mean to be born again? What is the spiritual state of people *before* being born again? Can our own efforts or decision help us to be born again? Why doesn't Nicodemus understand what Jesus is saying? Who causes the new birth to happen?

6. When God's Spirit comes to a person, he or she is born again. What important things does the Spirit then do in his life (Romans 8:14–16)? What changes in a person's life would one then expect to see?

Connect

1. What special blessings do we receive as a result of Christ's work (see Romans 8:14–17, John 3:16)? As a person begins to grasp the love and generosity of God, what is our natural response (Deuteronomy 6:5)? What are some specific ways we can express our love for God?

2. Romans 8 notes that the Spirit prompts us to call God "*Abba*." This is an Aramaic term a child of any age (especially grade-school-age) may use for his or her father, like "Dad," which is more intimate than "Father" *("Ab")* but not as childish as our term *Daddy*. What does this suggest about the degree of warmth, closeness, love, and respect God has established in our relationship to Him through Christ?

3. The New Age and human-potential movements tell people to look for divinity within themselves. Who are they saying is really "god?" How is this similar to the temptation Eve faced (Genesis 3:4–5)?

4. Why is it attractive to many people to feel that they have divinity in them? What inside of us shows the error of this idea (Romans 7:15–20)?

5. Deuteronomy 6 instructed God's people to write God's Word on their doorframes. How do Christians today visibly write God's Word on their doors, walls, cars, and clothes? Is this a good practice? Do these actions fulfill the intent of Deuteronomy 6 in and of themselves?

6. Why is it important to make God's Word a prominent part of our lives (see 2 Timothy 3:15–17)?

Vision

During This Week

1. Visit a Christian book store and pick out a bumper sticker, pin, door knocker, or wall hanging for display.
2. Memorize a key Bible verse that highlights God's love, such as John 3:16, Romans 8:39; 5:8, or a verse from Psalm 103.

Closing Worship

Read or sing together the following stanzas 1 and 4 of "Holy, Holy, Holy" (*LW* 168).

Holy, holy, holy,
Lord God Almighty!
Early in the morning our song shall rise to Thee.
Holy, holy, holy, merciful and mighty!
God in three Persons, blessed Trinity.

Holy, holy, holy,
Lord God Almighty!
All Thy works shall praise Thy name in earth and sky and sea.
Holy, holy, holy, merciful and mighty!
God in three Persons, blessed Trinity!

Scripture Lessons for Next Sunday

Read Deuteronomy 5:12–15, 2 Corinthians 4:5–12, and Mark 2:23–28 in preparation for the next session.

Session 2

Second Sunday after Pentecost

Deuteronomy 5:12–15; 2 Corinthians 4:5–12; Mark 2:23–28

Focus

Theme: *Remember Your Rescue!*

Law/Gospel Focus

We allow ourselves to be distracted by the demands and pleasures of life and to forget God's grace and salvation. As we do, our faith life weakens and becomes less important to us. God forgives us through Christ for our forgetting and leads us to remember His grace through regular worship, Scripture reading, and the Sacraments.

Objectives

By the power of the Holy Spirit working through God's Word we will

1. value experiences that will constantly remind us of how Christ rescued us from sin through the cross;
2. recognize the purpose and value of a weekly day of rest and worship;
3. recall times God has rescued us in the past and have hope in future times of difficulty.

Opening Worship

Pray together this litany adapted from Psalm 136.

Leader: Give thanks to the Lord, for He is good.
Participants: *His love endures forever.*
Leader: He rescued Israel from slavery in Egypt,
Participants: *His love endures forever.*
Leader: He gave Israel land as an inheritance,
Participants: *His love endures forever.*
Leader: By Christ He freed us from our enemies,

Participants: *His love endures forever.*
Leader: Give thanks to the Lord of lords,
Participants: *His love endures forever.*

Introduction

Our daughter looked forward to her birthday for months, even though she knew in advance all that would happen. We always remember our children's births in about the same way. Our closest friends from out of town visit and help us celebrate. Our daughter receives gifts. We reminisce about the day of her birth—how her dad almost passed out during childbirth, how she was critically ill and in intensive care, and the gut-wrenching feelings we had during the worst hours. We also recall our joy upon her recovery and our pleasure in having a new baby. We point out the exact time of her birth. (Grandma's hand-painted plaque on the wall notes the date and time.) We close the day with a circle prayer in which every member of the family thanks God for something about our birthday girl.

Remembering. That is what birthdays are all about. We all know the stories, but we need to tell and hear them again and again. Remembering a birthday demonstrates to people that their birthdays are important to us and that we care about and enjoy them.

Remembering is also a critical part of our lives as God's children. This is one important reason Christians set apart regular days and times for worship and teaching. We need to remember how God rescued us from sin, death, and the power of the devil. We need to tell and hear the stories again and again.

1. Think about your worship services. How do they enable you to remember God's rescue through Christ?

2. The Apostles' and Nicene Creeds are composed largely of memories of certain events (most of them from the earthly life of Jesus Christ). What things do we remember when we say these creeds?

Inform

Scan these summaries of the Scripture lessons for the Second Sunday after Pentecost.

Deuteronomy 5:12–15—God prescribed the weekly Sabbath for the good of His people. They were to do the two "r's"— rest from work and remember how God rescued them from slavery in Egypt.

2 Corinthians 4:5–12—We are always "under fire," weak, hard-pressed, and perplexed. But Christ rescues us and gives us His glory, power, hope, and life.

Mark 2:2–28—Christ is Lord of the Sabbath and created it to help people, not to burden them, as did the practice of the Pharisees.

These readings focus on how important it is for us to remember God's grace and how He rescued us through His Son's death on the cross from slavery to sin and death.

1. In order to make sure that Jews completely fulfilled God's command to rest *totally* on the Sabbath, rabbis wrote scores of additional regulations. For instance, the rabbis commanded that Jews were not to cover a pot, think about business affairs, or write more than one letter of the alphabet. They taught that a devout Jew could not do anything to help a person in pain (unless dangerously ill), even if the treatment involved no work. How did these rules cause people to lose sight of God's will? Were the Pharisees fulfilling the letter or the spirit of the Law? What had they forgotten about the purpose of the Sabbath (Mark 2:27)? What were the two main purposes of the Sabbath as God intended it (Deuteronomy 5:14–15)?

2. Why did Jesus allow his disciples to pick grain? What character trait does this suggest?

3. "Keep holy" means "to set apart." That is, to consider something different, to treat it as special, different from other things. When the Romans looked at the Jews on the Sabbath, would they have noticed that the Jews treated the day different than the other days of the week? What evidence of that would they have seen?

4. Before Christ God's people worshiped on the Sabbath, which was Saturday, the last day of the week. What did they remember about how God used the last day of the week (Genesis 2:2)? God's people after Christ worship primarily on Sunday, the first day of the week. What did the early Christians call this day (Revelation 1:10)? By doing this, what do we remember Christ did on the first day of the week (Luke 24:1–6)?

5. When the apostle Paul spoke of being "struck down" (2 Corinthians 4:8–9), he was not thinking of this in vague, philosophical terms. Instead, he remembered events during his missionary trips when he faced harm; yet the Lord rescued him. What such events from the book of Acts do you recall?

   On ship near the island of Malta (Acts 28)

   In jail in Caesarea (Acts 23)

   In prison in Philippi (Acts 16)

   Facing mobs in Iconium and Lystra (Acts 14)

6. When has God rescued you from trouble? How can Paul's (and our past) experiences give us hope?

7. What picture language does Paul use to describe our human weakness (2 Corinthians 4:7)? Why does he *not* use terms such as "jars of crystal" or "sculptures of marble" to describe it? What is the point of comparing us to "jars of clay?"

Connect

1. Jews remembered their rescue from slavery in Egypt. What slavery has God rescued us from?

2. We remember significant occasions through photos, reminiscing, reunions, and mementos. What do we say and do on Christmas to remember our Savior's coming to earth? What things do we do, see, and say at worship services to help us remember the person and work of Jesus Christ on our behalf? What things did Christ command us to *do* to remember Him?

3. Here are some common things people say about how they use their Sundays. How might you respond to each of them?
   - "I can worship God in nature."
   - "Sundays are my only day off, so it is the only day I can get errands done."

- "We use Sundays for family time."

- "I have to work overtime to pay our bills—especially our charge cards."

- "My faith in God is a very private affair."

What are these people forgetting?

4. Should worshiping and serving God be just a once-a-week thing? How can you make worship a daily experience for you?

5. The hardest times to remember God's grace and power to rescue are when … (See 2 Corinthians 4:8–9 if you need a hint.) What situations come to mind when you think of times when it is difficult to worship God?

Vision

During This Week

1. Choose something you can do, say, or look at this week to help you remember how God has rescued you.
2. Make a list of hard times God rescued you from in the past, both large and small. Put the list in a drawer or other place where you are likely to see it again. When you do, read it as a reminder of God's goodness to you.

Closing Worship

Read or sing together the following stanzas of "Oh, Bless the Lord, My Soul" (*LW* 457) or read Psalm 103 (in unison or antiphonally).

Oh, bless the Lord, my soul!
Let all in me combine
To aid my tongue to bless His name
Whose favor is divine.

Oh, bless the Lord, my soul!
Nor let His mercies lie
Forgotten in unthankfulness
And without praises die.

The Lord forgives my sins,
And He relieves my pain;
The Lord has healed my sicknesses
And made me whole again.

He crowns my life with love,
He ransoms from the grave;
He that redeemed my soul from hell
Has sov'reign pow'r to save.

He fills the poor with good;
He gives the suff'rers rest;
The Lord has judgments for the proud,
Relief for those oppressed.

His works and laws and ways
He made by Moses known
But showed the world His loving heart
In Christ, His only Son.

Scripture Lessons for Next Sunday

Read Genesis 3:9–15, 2 Corinthians 4:13–18, and Mark 3:20–35 in preparation for the next session.

Session 3

Third Sunday after Pentecost

Genesis 3:9–15; 2 Corinthians 4:13–18; Mark 3:20–35

Focus

Theme: ***There's a Battle On!***

Law/Gospel Focus

We often sense the damage our sin brings on ourselves or others, but we are quick to place the blame on others or tolerate the sin. Instead, we must admit our responsibility for our wrongdoing and our weakness in the face of temptation. Thankfully, Christ has come in power to free us from the grip of the enemy and make us part of God's family.

Objectives

By the power of the Holy Spirit working through God's Word we will

1. admit our wrongdoing and weakness in the face of temptation;
2. hate Satan and his ways and attack his work in this world;
3. better discern things in our lives which give Satan a grip on us;
4. thank God for freeing us from the power of sin and the devil through Jesus' death and resurrection, which gives us hope in the promise of eternal glory.

Opening Worship

Pray together this litany based on Psalm 27.

Leader: The Lord is the stronghold of my life—of whom shall I be afraid?

Participants: Though an army besiege me, I will not fear; even then will I be confident.

Leader: One thing I ask of the Lord, that I may dwell in His house.

Participants: and gaze upon the beauty of the Lord.

Leader: For in the day of trouble He will keep me safe in His dwelling; He will hide me;
Participants: Then I will sing and make music to the Lord.
Leader: Your face, Lord, I will seek. You have been my helper.
Participants: Though my father and mother forsake me, the Lord will receive me.
Leader: Teach me Your way, O Lord; lead me because of my oppressors.
Participants: I am confident of this: I will see the goodness of the Lord;
Leader: Wait for the Lord; be strong and take heart and wait for the Lord.

Introduction

The 1984 Winter Olympics were held in Sarajevo, Yugoslavia, with pomp, pageantry, and peace. But a decade later the city and the country were ravaged by civil war.

Nothing is the same when war starts. Friendships are torn, cities destroyed, people crippled and killed, jobs lost. Even surviving is hard, as people scratch to stay alive, avoid the enemy, and meet basic needs. No one can stay neutral, and hate increases as people are hurt more and more. As the United States learned in World War II, Korea, and Vietnam, even wars thousands of miles away demand that everyone come to grips with if, why, and how the war should be fought. All share its costs and consequences in the forms of economic losses, rationing, deaths, emotional trauma, labor, and fear. Anyone who tries to avoid these demands is trying to live in an unreal world and actually hinders the resolution of the conflict.

The Bible compares the Christian life to a war. Enemies seek to destroy us, sin's consequences plague us, we struggle to live as Christians should, and are called to obey the commands of our Ruler.

1. Do you think that your friends, family, the media, government, complex situations, and so forth have helped, or hindered, you in living an active Christian life?

2. What opposition to your faith have you faced?

Inform

Scan these summaries of the Scripture lessons for the Third Sunday after Pentecost.

Genesis 3:9–15—Adam and Eve did not want to own up to the fact that they had disobeyed God. Although God issued the curses which follow sin, He assured them that their offspring will crush the enemy who deceived Eve.

2 Corinthians 4:13–18—Although we are burdened by all the troubles which come with life in a sinful world, God renews us daily and assures Christ's followers of eternal glory.

Mark 3:20–35—Christ attacks Satan's evil kingdom by freeing people from evil and making them part of God's family.

These readings focus on how important it is for us to recognize evil attacks and fight back with the power of Jesus Christ.

1. Who is the serpent? What other names does the Bible use for him? Who is his "offspring" (Revelation 12:7–11)? All human beings are the woman's offspring, but only one stands out as the One who will crush Satan. Who is He?

2. Genesis suggests several consequences of sin, especially in 3:10, 12, 14, 15. What are they? One of them is "enmity" between her offspring and Satan. (*Satan* means "adversary," or "enemy," and "devil" means "slanderer.") *Enmity* means "hatred," or "hostility." What does this indicate that a Christian will experience in life?

3. Many people avoid taking responsibility for things they have done which are wrong or have hurt other people in some way. When God confronted Adam, did he take responsibility for what he had done? Whom did Adam blame? How does Eve answer God's question?

4. Sin and the conflict which follows it have ongoing effects on us. What are some of them (2 Corinthians 4:16–17)? Who is more powerful than sin and its consequences? What kind of future do Christians have to look forward to (verses 17–18)?

5. Who is the "strong man" in Jesus' parable (Mark 3:24–27)? What is his "house"? Who is the one who binds the strong man and robs his house?

6. What is one way Jesus robbed his "house" (Mark 3:22, 27). Why does Jesus call him the "strong man" but not "the strongest man" or "the weakling?" What kind of attitudes should Christians have toward the "strong man?"

7. The Jews called the prince of demons *Beelzebub* or *Beelzebul.* "Beelzebul" means "lord of the dung," a derisive parody of "Beelzebub," which means "lord of the (stinging) fly," which was a deity the Ekronites worshiped. What simple argument does Jesus use to explain why His actions make it clear that He opposes Satan?

8. Jesus refers to people who blaspheme against the Holy Spirit (Mark 3:29). This is sometimes called "the sin against the Holy Spirit." Study the context of this verse to help you understand what this is. Is Jesus referring to His weaker followers, or to His bitter opponents (3:22)? Are they asserting that Jesus' saving work and miracles are simply that of a misguided man, or that they are guided and powered by Satan himself? By saying that Jesus is doing Satan's work, are they actually rejecting the only source of salvation and consigning themselves to be lost forever?

Connect

1. Eve listened to the enemy. Christians sometimes listen to the words of the enemy and even invite him into their homes. Many forms of entertainment and friends promote sinful values, actions, attitudes, interests, and ways of speaking. This includes such things as sex outside marriage, violent behavior, occultism, New Age attitudes, profanity, and drug and alcohol abuse. What forms of music, magazines, movies, and TV shows promote these things?

2. The key battleground is in our minds. What is one important tool of Satan (Genesis 3:13)? Do Satan's temptations usually appear to be good and righteous, or to be obviously evil and Satanic? Some people say, "Mormons seem to be such good, religious people." Is this a reliable test? What is the better test? See 2 Corinthians 11:1–4, 13–15.

3. Since the Fall, the curse of sin has corrupted all of creation. In this fallen world, harmful consequences result when people break God's laws. There are many examples of this. What are some consequences of a promiscuous sexual life? What are common consequences of crimes? of harsh treatment of family members? of greed?

4. Why do we tend to blame other people (at least in part) rather than openly admit that our actions or attitudes were wrong? What can we do (especially during and after heated arguments) to ensure that we fully own up to things that are our fault?

5. Should a Christian *hate* anyone or anything? Who or what? Why? Whom should we especially strive to be at peace with (Mark 3:35)?

6. The word *devil* means "slanderer." On the basis of this, would one expect the non-Christian media to generally depict Christians and clergy as wise, upright people, or as unbalanced extremists who are behind the times? Why?

7. The picture language of "war" is used often in the Bible. Ephesians 6:10–18 lists the armor of God we can use in this war. What is our best defense (shield)? What is our primary weapon (sword)?

8. One prominent image of Jesus Christ in the book of Revelation is summed up in the words of "The Battle Hymn of the Republic:"

    Mine eyes have seen the glory of the coming of the Lord;
    He is trampling out the vintage where the grapes of wrath are stored;
    He hath loosed the fateful lighting of His terrible swift sword;
    His truth is marching on.
    Glory, glory! Hallelujah!
    Glory, glory! Hallelujah!
    Glory, glory! Hallelujah! His truth is marching on.

   Where and when did Christ's main triumph over sin and evil take place (Colossians 2:15)?

9. Throughout Jesus' ministry, is He just defending himself against Satan's attacks, or is he aggressively going on the offensive, attacking Satan's work? Are you or your church mostly defending yourself against the enemy, passively coasting, or aggressively attacking the enemy's work? What can a Christian do in the face of a …
   - magazine article that describes how science has proven that life evolved by chance out of nothing?
   - teacher who promotes all lifestyles and sexual behaviors as being good and equal?
   - video rental store with "adult" sections?
   - co-worker who implies that Christianity and the Bible is a myth?
   - daytime talk show that airs segments on homosexuality and other sinful sexual lifestyles?
   - teenager who listens to music that promotes profanity, sexual promiscuity, violence, or crime?
   - church member who tends to plant dissension in the congregation?

- community made up largely of unchurched people?
- friend who reads horoscopes, uses a Ouija board for fun, or has books on the power of the mind or reincarnation?

Vision

During This Week

1. Take a serious look at the music you hear and the videos and TV shows you watch. To what extent do they depict ungodly words, behavior, or situations? Dispose of those that encourage sex outside of marriage, violence, the occult, swearing, and ungodliness.

2. Write one or more letters to advertisers of TV shows that highlight the ungodly things mentioned above.

Closing Worship

Read or sing together the following stanzas of "Stand Up, Stand Up for Jesus" (*LW* 305).

Stand up, stand up for Jesus
As soldiers of the cross.
Lift high His royal banner;
It must not suffer loss.
From vict'ry unto vict'ry
His army He shall lead
Till ev'ry foe is vanquished
And Christ is Lord indeed.

Stand up, stand up for Jesus;
The strife will not be long;
This day the din of battle,
The next the victor's song.
The soldiers, overcoming,
Their crown of life shall see
And with the King of glory
Shall reign eternally.

Scripture Lessons for Next Sunday

Read Ezekiel 17:22–24, 2 Corinthians 5:1–10, and Mark 4:26–34 in preparation for the next session.

Session 4

Fourth Sunday after Pentecost

Ezekiel 17:22–24; 2 Corinthians 5:1–10; Mark 4:26–34

Focus

Theme: *God Grants Growth!*

Law/Gospel Focus

Apart from God, our spiritual lives are dead and our emotional growth is stilted. But through Christ God provides life and power to grow both spiritually and emotionally until we become mature and finally receive fullness of life and immortality in our heavenly dwelling after death.

Objectives

By the power of the Holy Spirit working through God's Word we will

1. appreciate the importance of becoming emotionally and spiritually mature by God's measure rather than by human standards;
2. better discern the difference between the world's idea of maturity and God's model;
3. trust God to supply spiritual growth, which we are helpless to muster on our own;
4. give thanks to God for the eternal life Christ won for us through His death on the cross.

Opening Worship

Speak together the following adapted from Psalms 1 and 52.

Leader: Blessed is the one who does not live like an ungodly person,

Participants: But delights in the Word of the Lord, and always reflects on it.

Leader: He is like a tree planted by streams of water, which yields fruit in season and does not wither.
Participants: Whatever he does prospers.
Leader: Not so the wicked! They are like clippings that the wind blows away.
Participants: Therefore the wicked will not stand in the judgment.
Leader: For the Lord watches over the righteous, but the way of the wicked will perish.
Participants: I am like an olive tree flourishing in the house of God;
Leader: I trust in God's unfailing love for ever and ever.
All: Lord, I will praise You forever for what You have done; in You I will hope, for You are good.

Introduction

A mushroom can spring up, fully grown, in a lawn overnight. But an orange or walnut tree takes years to grow to full height and fruitfulness. Which would you rather have in your yard, and on your table at harvest time?

In our microwave, fast-food, instant-coffee society, we often get frustrated when we can't have exactly what we want, right away. And we become depressed by illness, losses, and deaths over which we have no control, and for which humanity has no solutions.

God uses these situations to impress upon us our own weakness, spiritual corruption, and physical decay. We desperately need God to provide the immortality we desire, and the emotional and spiritual growth we need. God was up to the task. He sent Jesus to live a perfect life on our behalf, suffer on the cross the punishment we deserved because of our sin, and rise victorious from the grave, proclaiming victory for us over sin and death. His power, wisdom, and grace is more than sufficient to meet our every need.

What situations in your life, or in your home, work, church, society, or in a friend's life, seem out of control?

God is up to the task of providing you help, strength, and hope no matter what circumstances you may face. Keep in mind He sacrificed His only Son so that you might face the ultimate consequence of sin—death—with joy.

Inform

Scan these summaries of the Scripture lessons for the Fourth Sunday after Pentecost.

Ezekiel 17:22–24—Just as God can increase or hinder the growth of a tree, so He can create growth in people.

2 Corinthians 5:1–10—While we have pain and discouragement due to physical weaknesses, we can look forward with hope to the day we go to live eternally with Jesus.

Mark 4:26–34—Just as God causes plants to grow, so He causes His kingdom to grow.

These readings focus on the power of God to give spiritual, emotional and physical life.

1. Do the verses in Ezekiel and Mark emphasize what people (the "trees") do, or what God does? Can we find salvation from sin and death on our own, or must we depend on God to do it all, through the cross of Christ? What does this tell us about God's character?

2. Throughout the Bible, trees or plants are often used as a symbol for people (note Psalm 1). Why would God want to bring down a "tall tree" (a person or nation who is prosperous by human measure)? Why would He want to make a "low tree" grow tall (become strong and mature)?

3. What is the "earthly tent" we live in (2 Corinthians 5:1, 6)? Why does Paul call it a "tent" instead of a "house" or "palace?"

4. What is there about life in this body that makes us "groan and [be] burdened" (5:4)? What do people do in the areas of medicine, exercise, recreation, and home life to ease these feelings?

5. How does our mortality affect us? How does Jesus relieve us from these ailing mortal bodies?

Connect

1. Ezekiel and Mark speak of the growth of God's kingdom. What two kinds of growth are especially important (see Ephesians 4:13 and 6:19–20)?

2. Christian maturity is different from what the world sees as maturity. We must learn God's kind of maturity in order to "grow up" properly. Read Ephesians 4:25–32. What are some marks of Christian maturity?

3. We may feel frustrated when our spiritual lives seem to languish and old sinful habits are tough to beat. Where can one find hope to overcome this (Mark 4:27)? What means does God use to do so?

4. It sometimes seems that our work for the Lord is futile—Sunday school children may be wild, or our church may be struggling to grow. What kind of encouragement does Mark 4:27–28 and Isaiah 55:10–11 have for frustrated Christian servants?

5. Paul describes the earthly body as a "tent" and the resurrection body (which God will give us after death) as an "eternal house/home." Which is more desirable to live in—a tent or a house? Why? Knowing this, what kinds of attitudes, or feelings, can we have as we look forward to death?

Vision

During This Week

1. Write a note of encouragement to a Sunday school teacher, church worker, Christian leader, or tired parent. Remind them of God's power to bring growth in "futile" situations and assure them of your concern, thoughts, and prayers. You may also wish to offer them some specific help.

2. Pick two conversations you have in the coming week (or had last week) in which there are strong feelings, tension, or sharp words. Write down, or review in your mind, specific things you said or did. Compare them to the marks of maturity mentioned in Ephesians 4. Confess sinful actions and words. Be assured of Christ's forgiveness. Pray that the Holy Spirit would enable you to demonstrate increasing maturity.

Closing Worship

Read or sing together stanza 4 of "How Great Thou Art" (*LW* 519).

When Christ shall come with shout of acclamation
And take me home, what joy shall fill my heart!
Then I shall bow in humble adoration
And there proclaim: "My God, how great Thou art!"
Then sings my soul, my Savior God, to Thee,
How great Thou art! How great Thou art!
Then sings my soul, my Savior God, to Thee,
How great Thou art! How great Thou art!

Scripture Lessons for Next Sunday

Read Job 38:1–11, 2 Corinthians 5:14–21, and Mark 4:35–41 in preparation for the next session.

Session 5

Fifth Sunday after Pentecost

Job 38:1–11; 2 Corinthians 5:14–21; Mark 4:35–41

Focus

Theme: *God Still Creates Today!*

Law/Gospel Focus

Because of sin—our own and the sins of others—we face trouble and pain. We may ask, "Where is God? Doesn't He care?" God has not turned His back on us. His great love for us led His only Son to the cross to suffer and die for us. Jesus proclaimed victory for us over sin when He rose from the dead. God assures us in His Word that nothing can separate us from His love in Christ. His love for us enables us to face troubles with the confidence that He is with us always.

Objectives

By the power of the Holy Spirit working through God's Word we will

1. acknowledge God's creative and re-creative power;
2. remember that God cares for us in our troubles, and trust His mercy for help;
3. seek God's faith-strengthening power offered freely through His means of grace;
4. share Jesus' love with others as they face troubles.

Opening Worship

Join together in this litany adapted from Psalm 8.

Leader: O Lord, our Lord, how majestic is Your name in all the earth!

Participants: From the lips of children You have ordained praise, to silence Your enemies.

Leader: When I consider Your heavens, the stars and planets which You have set in place,

Participants: what is man that You care for him?
Leader: You made him a little lower than the heavenly beings and crowned him with glory and honor.
Participants: You made us ruler over the works of Your hands; over all the world and its animals;
All: O Lord, our Lord, how majestic is Your name in all the earth!

Introduction

Doesn't God care? Whenever troubles and pain come into our lives, we cry out to God for help. When our prayers are not answered the way we want, and as soon as we want, we may feel God is ignoring us, or that He even takes pleasure in seeing us writhe.

Many people throughout history have imagined this kind of detached, apathetic God. God is like a watchmaker, they say. He made and "wound up" the world, then stepped away to let it run on its own. They didn't expect God to really hear people or to intervene on their behalf.

Does God care? Is He listening to us? Is He active in intervening for us, or is He still resting after His six days of hard work creating this world?

What troubles have come upon you or people you know which have made you wonder if God really cares?

Inform

Scan these summaries of the Scripture lessons for the Fifth Sunday after Pentecost.

Job 38:1–11—God reacts angrily to the ignorance and pride of Job and his friends, and He challenges Job to see if he can match His wisdom and creative power.

2 Corinthians 5:14–21—God did not abandon people when they became His enemies due to sin. Instead, He reconciled us through Christ's atoning sacrifice and made us new creations.

Mark 4:35–41—Jesus demonstrates His power over creation by stilling the storm-driven waves and wind.

These readings focus on the creative and the re-creative power God uses on our behalf, both past and present.

1. God asks Job a lot of questions, and Job has no answers. Why not? What is Job likely feeling and thinking during this interrogation?

2. What does God want Job to learn, think, or do differently as a result of this encounter?

3. God asks Job, "Where were you when… [I created the world]?" Of course, Job wasn't there at that time. But Jesus' disciples were there when He stopped the storm. How did they react to this demonstration of Jesus' power (Mark 4:41)?

4. God tells Job that He "shut up the sea behind doors when it burst forth." Mark records the night that Jesus shut up the sea behind doors to keep it from swamping the disciples' boat. What does Jesus' miracle tell us about Himself?

5. What other indications of Jesus' creative and re-creative power are evident in the scriptural accounts of His person and work?

Connect

1. The disciples accused Jesus of apathy when they said, "Don't you care if we drown?" Why did they think that Jesus didn't care? Why did Job not understand God (Job 38:2)? What other things lead people today to feel that God doesn't care? Does Christ care? How does He show it today? What does Jesus invite us to do as we face troubles? See Matthew 11:28.

2. The disciples asked themselves "Who is this?" after seeing this miracle. What answer did they eventually receive (see Matthew 16:15–16 and John 20:28)?

3. How do you think Jesus' miracle may have affected the disciples' level of worry and faith? How did it likely affect their prayer life and reaction to opposition? How did it affect their goal and purpose in life (2 Corinthians 5:15)?

4. God's power extends beyond inanimate things to people. What creative power does Christ use in people's lives today (2 Corinthians 5:17)?

5. In what ways are believers in Christ made "new" in their relationship with God? in their personal lives? in their dealings with other people?

6. The key word the apostle uses to describe our new relationship with God is *reconciled* (2 Corinthians 5:18–21). Before reconciliation, what marks people's relationship with God (see Romans 5:9–11 and recall our discussion of enmity from Genesis 3:15 in session 3)?

7. What does it mean to be "reconciled" with God? What takes the place of enmity and hostility? What does God create in believers (2 Corinthians 5:21)?

8. Who took the first step in reconciliation—God or people (2 Corinthians 5:18–19)? Does this suggest bitterness and apathy on God's part, or mercy and grace? This belief is unique to Christianity, because non-Christian religions always speak of people doing the reconciling. What key means does God use to bring about reconciliation (2 Corinthians 5:19, 21)?

9. You have been reconciled with God through Christ's death on the cross. What is the next step the Holy Spirit enables and motivates you to do (2 Corinthians 5:19–20)? What are some specific ways you can do this?

Vision

During This Week

1. Who can you tell about becoming reconciled to God through Christ? Plan a time or way you can approach a particular person to tell him or her about Christ.

2. Memorize 2 Corinthians 5:17, "Therefore, if anyone is in Christ, he is a new creation; the old has gone, the new has come!" or 2 Corinthians 5:21, "God made Him who had no sin to be sin for us, so that in Him we might become the righteousness of God" by taping it to your car dashboard, home mirror, or refrigerator and reading it aloud whenever you see it.

3. Do you find yourself feeling a lot of guilt and regrets? If so, take a sheet of paper and lay it sideways on a table. On the left side, write the word *God,* and on the right, your own name. In the middle list the sins which you often mull over, regret, or feel guilty about. Then tear out the middle and burn or shred it. Tape the two sides together as a reminder that the sins and barriers between you and God are gone and you are reconciled with Him through faith in Christ Jesus. Add hearts, crosses, rainbows, or other symbols to symbolize the new love and closeness with God that Christ has brought to you.

Closing Worship

Read or sing together "Renew Me, O Eternal Light" (*LW* 373).

Renew me, O eternal Light,
And let my heart and soul be bright,
Illumined with the light of grace
That issues from Your holy face.

Remove the pow'r of sin from me
And cleanse all my impurity
That I may have the strength and will
Temptations of the flesh to still.

Create in me a new heart, Lord,
That gladly I obey Your Word.
Let what You will be my desire,
And with new life my soul inspire.

Grant that I only You may love
And seek those things which are above
Till I behold You face to face,
O Light eternal, through Your grace.

Scripture Lessons for Next Sunday

Read Lamentations 3:22–33, 2 Corinthians 8:1–14, and Mark 5:21–24, 35–43 in preparation for the next session.

Session 6

Sixth Sunday after Pentecost

Lamentations 3:22–33; 2 Corinthians 8:1–14;
Mark 5:21–24, 35–43

Focus

Theme: *God Turns Grief into Joy*

Law/Gospel Focus

We often find ourselves overwhelmed by feelings of hopelessness, sadness, and grief as we face troubles and hardships. But God in Christ came to earth to die on the cross for our sins and in so doing conquered the cause—sin—and the ultimate effect—death. In Christ, we can face all things with joy and confidence because we know that nothing can separate us from His love, which earned for us eternal life.

Objectives

By the power of the Holy Spirit working through God's Word we will

1. acknowledge that God does not delight in the grief that because of sin may come upon us, but shows compassion and unfailing love;
2. affirm that God will and does act on our behalf;
3. demonstrate joy in knowing that nothing can or will separate us from God's love for us in Jesus.

Opening Worship

Pray together the following adapted from the Old Testament reading for the Sixth Sunday after Pentecost.

Leader: The Lord's great love and His compassion never fail.

Participants: They are new every morning; great is Your faithfulness.

Leader: The Lord is my portion; therefore I will wait for Him.

Participants: He is good to those who hope in Him, and who seek Him;
Leader: it is good to wait quietly for the salvation of the Lord.
Participants: He does not willingly bring affliction or grief to people.
Leader: Though He brings grief, He will show compassion, so great is His unfailing love.
Participants: I call this to mind and therefore I have hope.

Introduction

Happiness is ... a big bank account, a comfortable life, a perfect spouse, sweet children, a good job?

Often when people accumulate all the things they think will make them happy, they still find life empty and unfulfilling. "I wish I could go back to when we were young," they say, "we didn't have much then, but we were happier."

Joy is not a product of how rich (or poor), comfortable (or uncomfortable), or socially active (or inactive) a person is. God in Christ provides us peace and joy no matter what our external condition is, no matter what hardship we must endure.

1. What times in your life have been the most joyful? Was the joy connected primarily to the material things you had? What was it related to?

2. Think of a time in your life you might consider joyless. What occurred to once again give you joy?

Inform

Scan these summaries of the Scripture lessons for the Sixth Sunday after Pentecost.

Lamentations 3:22–33—Although we must endure the consequences of our sin and the sins of others, God's love for the repentant sinner never ceases; His mercies never cease. The Lord will provide salvation to all who turn to Him in faith.

2 Corinthians 8:1–14—The Macedonian churches were so full of God's grace that they did not allow their poverty and affliction to keep them from giving joyfully their money and themselves to God and those in need.

Mark 5:21–24,35–43—Jairus trusted in Christ and His power, and Jesus replaced his grief with joy by raising his daughter from the dead.

These readings focus on the Lord's power and compassion to replace our grief with joy.

1. Lamentations 3 describes people who are feeling grief and disgrace. What should a person do in trying times such as these (verses 25–26)? What are the implications for us as we face the consequences of our sin or the sins of others?

2. How is God described in Lamentations 3:22, 23, 25, 32? How do these verses provide hope and joy in the midst of despair?

3. How does Jairus show his faith in Jesus Christ during his time of grief (Mark 5:23)? What do you think Jairus saw in Jesus that prompted such great faith?

4. Jesus had power over life and death. How do you think Jairus responded to Jesus raising his daughter from the dead? How does faith in Jesus' power over life and death affect us as we anticipate physical death? How does God enable us to respond?

5. The Macedonian churches experienced severe trial and extreme poverty. What feelings or attitudes would you expect them to have as a result? What did they have instead (2 Corinthians 8:2)? What added power made this possible (8:1)? What is stronger—God's grace and joy, or trial and poverty?

6. In what six important parts of Christian living does God by His grace through faith enable and motivate us to excel (2 Corinthians 8:7)?

7. Some people approach serving God and others as a tedious duty. What attitude toward giving did the Macedonians have (2 Corinthians 8:2, 4)?

Connect

1. The author of Lamentations and his people lost everything—homes, freedom, temple worship, food, health, friends, and family. What losses have you faced in recent years—job, health, loved ones, husband, wife, family harmony?

2. God allows us to experience grief, especially when it comes as a consequence of our disobeying or distrusting Him. But what always follows the grief for all repentant sinners? What is God's "last word" (Lamentations 3:32)?

3. The writers mention three important things to do when facing grief. What are they (Lamentations 3:26, Mark 5:36)? What does it mean to "wait quietly" for God's salvation? When it comes, what do we experience in place of grief?

4. How did Jairus' relatives react to the loss of his daughter (Mark 5:36–39)? How and why was Jairus' reaction different? Why did they laugh when Jesus said that the child was only sleeping?

5. Jesus said, "Don't be afraid; just believe." Are fear and faith opposites? Why? How does faith melt fear? Is Jesus encouraging Jairus to have faith in Christ, to have faith that the child will become well, or both?

6. Jesus often sees things differently than the world does. In Jesus' view, what is the death of a believer like (Mark 5:39)? This is a common attitude among believers (see 1 Corinthians 15:51, 1 Thessalonians 4:13, Acts 7:60). What does Jesus imply when He pictures death as being like sleep?

7. We find a lesson of "God's Math" in 2 Corinthians 8:2. It reads "Joy + Poverty = ________." One would expect the sum of this math problem to be "joyful poverty," or just "hopeless poverty." What did the Macedonians get when through faith in Jesus they added joy and poverty?

8. The Macedonians were exceptional givers in many ways. What did they give along with their money (2 Corinthians 8:5)? What does it mean that they "gave themselves?" What did they say or do that shows they "gave themselves?" How might God, who has showered us with His abundant grace, enable us to give ourselves to others (individually and as a congregation)?

Vision

During This Week

1. Write a check to LCMS World Relief (P.O. Box 66861, St. Louis, MO 63166-9810) or a similar organization to help supply what others need. You may wish to follow the Macedonians' example by giving more than you thought reasonable in the past.
2. Write a note of encouragement to a person who has lost something dear to them in the past few years (such as a loved one, health, job, home, husband, wife, family harmony, etc). Assure them of God's, and your own, love and compassion.

Closing Worship

Read or sing together stanzas 1 and 6 of "We Give You But Your Own" (*LW* 405).

We give You but Your own
In any gifts we bring;
All that we have is Yours alone,
A trust from You, our King.

And we believe Your Word,
Though dim our faith, it's true:
What we do for Your people, Lord,
We do it all for You.

Scripture Lessons for Next Sunday

Read Ezekiel 2:1–5, 2 Corinthians 12:7–10, and Mark 6:1–6 in preparation for the next session.

Session 7

Seventh Sunday after Pentecost

Ezekiel 2:1–5; 2 Corinthians 12:7–10; Mark 6:1–6

Focus

Theme: *Facing the Ridicule of Skeptics*

Law/Gospel Focus

Even though we know the truth of Scripture, we can find ourselves giving in to those who ridicule us and our faith in order to pacify them or to avoid conflict. God through Christ Jesus offers us forgiveness when we fail to confess Jesus Christ is Lord and provides us the power to stand strong and overcome our inhibitions and fears.

Objectives

By the power of the Holy Spirit working through God's Word we will

1. confess our often weak or nonexistent confession of faith in Jesus Christ our Lord and Savior and the truth God provides to all in His Word;
2. rely on the power of Christ's love when we are weak or under attack;
3. resolve to live lives devoted to making disciples for Christ, even when others reject or insult us.

Opening Worship

Join together in this prayer adapted from Psalms 27 and 28.

Leader: Almighty God, do not drag me away with those who speak cordially with their neighbors but harbor malice in their hearts.

Participants: Though my father and mother forsake me, the Lord will receive me.

Leader: In the day of trouble He will keep me safe in His dwelling;
Participants: He will set me high over the enemies who surround me;
Leader: then I will sing and make music to the Lord.
Participants: The Lord is my strength and my shield; my heart trusts in Him, and I am helped.
Leader: The Lord is our strength, a fortress of salvation;
Participants: Save us, bless us, be our shepherd and carry us forever.

Introduction

"I don't know why you bother teaching Sunday school every week," Tom told Sharon, "I think it's a waste of time."

"I don't think so," she answered (for about the 100th time).

"Besides, all the church wants is your money. It's full of hypocrites, I know that for sure."

"You know how I feel about the church," Sharon pleaded. "You don't have to keep battering me with your criticisms every week. You know it makes me feel bad."

1. Can you remember any instance when one of your acquaintances, friends, or family members said or inferred that your faith was a myth or your service for God a waste?

2. What effect does criticism have on people?

Inform

Scan these summaries of the Scripture lessons for the Seventh Sunday after Pentecost.

Ezekiel 2:1–5—God sends Ezekiel to speak His words of judgment to the Israelites, knowing that they will be stubborn and many will not listen.

2 Corinthians 12:7–10—Paul is given something to torment Him in order to keep him from becoming conceited. By this, he learns that hardship and weakness is good, because only Christ's power makes him strong at those times.

Mark 6:1–6—When Jesus comes to His hometown to teach, the people do not accept Him. Instead they question His power and authority.

These readings focus on how God gives His people strength and encouragement even as they face stubbornness and insults by unbelievers.

1. How did the Lord describe the people to whom he was sending Ezekiel (2:3–4)? How might these words also describe people to whom God might send you to proclaim His love and forgiveness through Jesus?

2. How did the people in Jesus' hometown react to His ministry and teaching (Mark 6:3)? What does it mean that they were "offended" by Him?

3. Did Jesus do no miracles in Nazareth because he didn't want to? because He didn't have enough power? What was the real problem (Mark 6:6)? Is God more willing to give than people are to receive, or the other way around? How is this true today?

4. What did Ezekiel, Paul, and Jesus all have in common (2 Corinthians 12:10)?

5. Why did Paul delight in weaknesses and hardships (2 Corinthians 12:9)? Why is it often hard for us to delight in weakness?

6. What temptation did Paul face as a result of having had great revelations from God (12:7)? Why is this such a dangerous temptation, especially for a Christian leader?

Connect

1. Why did the Lord warn Ezekiel in advance that the people to whom he preached would be stubborn and rebellious? When a Christian today leads a life devoted to the Lord and to witnessing for Him, should he or she expect people to accept and tolerate her/him?

2. The response of the Nazarenes to Jesus was, in a nutshell, "So who do you think you are anyway—certainly *not* a prophet from God!" Israelites reacted to Ezekiel the same way. What conviction kept him going (Ezekiel 2:3)? When you are ridiculed for your faith, what similar conviction can keep you going (Matthew 28:19)?

3. People in Nazareth were offended by Jesus' words. When someone is offended by what we say, is it important to always apologize? Why or why not?

4. How can a person distinguish between criticism that is just and accurate and that which is unjust and unwarranted?

5. To what kinds of temptations are you most vulnerable? Select those from this list and underline them.
   - pride
   - bitterness—finding it too hard to forgive someone
   - insincerity
   - not following through on promise to people or God
   - immorality
   - not telling the whole truth
   - prejudice
   - taking advantage of others
   - apathy (showing little compassion)
   - cowardice when criticized
   - anger
   - (other) ______________________

What could you do in order to receive help to deal with these?

6. What is God's attitude to human weakness and vulnerability to temptation? (Impatience? Despise it? Turn away from people who give in? Compassion? Concern and aid?) Did God spurn Paul, withdraw his apostleship, become impatient with him, or compassionately take steps to help Paul? What does this suggest about God's character?

7. Fill in the blanks:
   When I am weak, Christ is ____________ in me.
   When I am ____________, Christ is ____________ in me.
   Check the best answer:
   I am most in spiritual danger when
   ______ I feel strong enough to handle temptation.
   ______ I feel too weak to handle temptation alone.

Vision

During This Week

1. Review some of the troubles, weaknesses and hardships in your life in past years. What good character traits or spiritual maturity did God enable you to receive from these?

2. Share God's love in Christ with a person who has rejected this message before. Be assured that God's Word will accomplish its purpose.

Closing Worship

Read or sing together "Have No Fear, Little Flock" (*LW* 410).

Have no fear, little flock;
Have no fear, little flock,
For the Father has chosen
To give you the Kingdom;
Have no fear, little flock!

Have good cheer, little flock;
Have good cheer, little flock,
For the Father will keep you
In His love forever;
Have good cheer, little flock!

Praise the Lord high above;
Praise the Lord high above,
For He stoops down to heal you,
Uplift and restore you;
Praise the Lord high above!

Thankful hearts raise to God;
Thankful hearts raise to God,
For He stays close beside you,
In all things works with you;
Thankful hearts raise to God!

Scripture Lessons for Next Sunday

Read Amos 7:10–15, Ephesians 1:3–14, and Mark 6:7–13 in preparation for the next session.

Session 8

Eighth Sunday after Pentecost

Amos 7:10–15; Ephesians 1:3–14; Mark 6:7–13

Focus

Theme: *Chosen and Equipped for God's Work*

Law/Gospel Focus

Because of sin people are separated from God and would be lost eternally. But God in His love for all people sent His Son Jesus to live a perfect life on their behalf and suffer the punishment they deserved because of their sin. God calls all people through the Gospel to faith in Christ Jesus so they might receive His forgiveness and serve Him eternally.

Objectives

By the power of the Holy Spirit working through God's Word we will

1. recognize that God has called us to faith through the Gospel to be His children and servants;
2. thank God for His overwhelming generosity and love for us;
3. become increasingly willing to take risks as a result of faith in God's promises and obedience to His commands to serve Him;
4. discover ways to serve God, regardless of how weak or ill-equipped we may feel.

Opening Worship

Pray together the following adapted from Psalm 16.

Leader: I said to the Lord,

Participants: "You are my Lord; apart from You I have no good thing."

Leader: The saints are glorious; I delight in them.

Participants: But those who run after other gods will have more and more sorrows.

Leader: Lord, You have assigned me a delightful portion; You made my lot secure.
Participants: I will praise the Lord, who counsels me;
Leader: I have set the Lord always before me, I will not be shaken;
Participants: Therefore I am glad and I rejoice.
Leader: You have made known to me the path of life;
Participants: You will fill me with joy and eternal pleasure.

Introduction

Democratic governments such as the United States and Canada emphasize the critical importance of elections. Yet only a handful of the tens of thousands of "public servants" are elected—far too few to plan and to administrate the many functions of government. Where do the rest of the workers come from?

Perhaps the most important function of an elected official is that of choosing and appointing his workers. Officials choose cabinet members, judges, ambassadors, administrators, lawyers, writers, budget directors, tax collectors, and host of varied workers. These workers carry out the general directives of elected officials.

Jesus Christ came to earth as the "Head" of a major body. He has chosen, and still continues to choose, servants to speak for Him and do His work. The Bible describes all Christians as ambassadors who speak for God and as servants who do His bidding.

1. What is the difference between seeing oneself as just a child of God, versus seeing yourself as a God's child *and* as His ambassador? If a person takes seriously his or her role as God's ambassador, how would this show in his actions and words?

2. If every Christian performed well as God's ambassador, what difference would this make in the church at large (and in your congregation)?

Inform

Scan these summaries of the Scripture lessons for the Eighth Sunday after Pentecost.

Amos 7:10–15—God sends Amos to warn Israel. He is bold enough to prophesy in the king's own backyard, risking the wrath of the very king and people he came to warn.

Ephesians 1:3–14—Paul describes for the Ephesians God's enormous, outgoing, unilateral and unconditional love for all people through Christ. We are God's children, redeemed from sin, death, and the power of the devil by the blood of Jesus shed on the cross.

Mark 6:7–13—Jesus sends out the Twelve, equipping them for the task of service and promising that God will provide all they need.

These readings focus on how God chooses people to be His children and equips them to work and speak in His name.

1. Where did Amos prophesy and what person did he prophesy against? What risk was Amos taking by doing this?

2. Amos wasn't born into a family of prophets. Why did he become a prophet?

3. Does Ephesians emphasize what we should do for God, or what God has done for us? What verb tense does Paul use to tell us of God's generosity to us (1:6, 7, 9)? Why?

4. What key words are repeated more than once in Ephesians 1? What is the significance of the repetition of these words?

5. Why did we become God's children? Who took the initiative to bring this about (1:4, 5, 11)?

6. What did Jesus send out the Twelve to do (Mark 6:12–13)? What was significant or unique about the way they were to accomplish their assigned tasks?

Connect

1. When we begin to realize the overwhelming grace and love God gives us, what will naturally flow from us (Ephesians 1:3, 6, 12, 14)?

2. What means does God use to bring grace to us (1:13)? Keeping this in mind, why did God count it so important to send Amos, and the Twelve, to speak His Word? Why does God send us who have experienced the abundance of His grace into the world?

3. What power does the Lord give us to assure us of His promises and to help us serve Him (Ephesians 1:13–14)?

4. Did Amos and the Twelve get their authority from the religious leaders of the day? What was the source of their authority? Who has received the authority and responsibility from God to share Christ today with the world (Peter 2:9)?

5. Serving Christ often involves taking small risks. Read the list below. Which items have you or someone else you know felt? What can encourage you to take the risk to serve God? See 2 Timothy 3:15–17.
   - "If I let my co-workers know I'm a sincere Christian and take a stand for my faith when I need to, I could get reprimanded by my boss."
   - "If I gave more than 2 or 3 percent of my income to church or to the poor, I wouldn't have enough for my needs."
   - "If I visited someone for the church, I probably couldn't think of anything to say, and I'd get embarrassed."
   - "If I came to church or Bible study more often, my family would get upset."
   - "My church needs Sunday school and Bible study teachers, but I'm afraid I wouldn't do it well."
   - "I'm not exactly a model Christian; if I talked about sin and God to any of my friends or neighbors, they'd point the finger right back at me."

Vision

During This Week

1. Read the different kinds of service to God in Romans 12:3–8, 1 Corinthians 12:27–31, and Ephesians 4:11–13. Resolve to serve in one or two of these (or similar) ways.
2. Write a one-paragraph statement of what God has and will do for us, based on Ephesians 1:3–14. Reflect on it and plan to share it with one person in the next two weeks.

Closing Worship

Read or sing together "Take My Life, O Lord, Renew" (*LW* 404).

Take my life, O Lord, renew,
Consecrate my heart to You;
Take my moments and my days;
Let them sing Your ceaseless praise.

Take my hands and let them do
Works that show my love for You;
Take my feet and lead their way,
Never let them go astray.

Take my voice and let me sing
Praises to my Savior King;
Take my lips and keep them true,
Filled with messages from You.

Take my silver and my gold,
All is Yours a thousand fold;
Take my intellect, and use
Ev'ry pow'r as You shall choose.

Make my will Your holy shrine,
It shall be no longer mine.
Take my heart, it is Your own;
It shall be Your royal throne.

Take my love; my Lord, I pour
At Your feet its treasure store;
Take my self, Lord, let me be
Yours alone eternally.

Scripture Lessons for Next Sunday

Read Jeremiah 23:1–6, Ephesians 2:13–22, and Mark 6:30–34 in preparation for the next session.

Session 9

Ninth Sunday after Pentecost

Jeremiah 23:1–6; Ephesians 2:13–22; Mark 6:30–34

Focus

Theme: *One Shepherd—One Flock*

Law/Gospel Focus

Because people are by nature sinful, we are divided, separated, alone, and in need. People are at odds with God, families break apart, churches divide into factions, and death separates. As a result, lives are filled with worry, fear, loneliness, and helplessness. But God reconciled us to Himself through His Son's death on the cross, making us part of His flock. Our Good Shepherd makes us one heart and mind and unites us into one flock as the Spirit works through God's Word to strengthen our faith, transforming worry, fear, loneliness, and helplessness into safety, companionship, peace, and joy.

Objectives

By the power of the Holy Spirit working through God's Word we will

1. confess Christ as our Good Shepherd who delivers us from fear and from sinful habits that prompt disunity, and who provides for our needs;
2. affirm the key to unity—that just as God graciously accepts us because of His Son's sacrificial death on the cross, so we are empowered and motivated by His love to graciously accept others;
3. explore ways to strengthen unity between God's people.

Opening Worship

Pray together the following adapted from Psalm 133.

Leader: How good and pleasant it is when brothers live together in unity!

Participants: It is like precious oil poured on Aaron's head,
Leader: running down his beard, down upon the collar of his robes.
Participants: It is as if the dew of Hermon were falling on Mount Zion.
Leader: For there the Lord bestows His blessing,
Participants: even life forevermore.

Introduction

Church potlucks had become an ugly source of conflict at St. Peter's. One group of parishioners insisted that they use Styrofoam and plastic plates and cups. The other group demanded they use paper plates and cups exclusively. The difference grew from disagreement to argument and then to battle. The lines were clearly drawn, and both sides were fighting for the same territory.

Only a year or two passed before the situation became intolerable. Most of the people wanting to use paper plates and cups soon transferred to another church, wondering how they could ever have been drawn into such an unfriendly congregation.

Sound like a silly reason for disharmony? Well, every year events such as these can cause discord in a congregation.

1. What divisions have you heard of (or experienced) in various churches? What kinds of conflicts and arguments took place? What happened to people as a result?

2. Sometimes there are fights that center on seemingly insignificant things, such as the kind of products to use at a potluck. What more significant issues may lie beneath the surface (and perhaps never openly acknowledged)?

Inform

Scan these summaries of the Scripture lessons for the Ninth Sunday after Pentecost.

Jeremiah 23:1–6—The Lord compares His people to sheep who are scattered and afraid when they have no good shepherd to lead them in God's ways. But He will send one who will lead them to righteousness and salvation.

Ephesians 2:13–22—Sin has led people farther and farther from God and other people. But God graciously reconciled us with Himself through Christ Jesus' death on the cross, and He unites us with other people who have received the gift of faith.

Mark 6:30–34—Jesus Christ cares for confused people, as a shepherd does his sheep, and brings people together under His charge.

These readings focus on how God brings peace to us by reconciling us to Himself and uniting us into one household—His church.

1. Without good leaders ("shepherds," i.e., pastors), what happens to God's people ("sheep")? Why? See Jeremiah 23:2, 4.

2. What happens to God's people when there are good "shepherds" (Jeremiah 23:3, 6, and the opposites of things listed in 23:2, 4)?

3. Jeremiah describes the one who will gather God's people. What four titles does Jeremiah use to describe Him (23:4, 5, 6)? (Three of these names are capitalized in the NIV.) What is the significance of these titles?

4. The key phrase in Ephesians 2 is *in Christ* ("in Him"), which appears six times in verses 13–22. What six things happen "in [through] Him?" How are these six things still meaningful for us today?

5. Mark 6 shows how Jesus fulfilled Jeremiah's prophecy. Who is gathering around Jesus? Where are they coming from? How does Jesus respond?

Connect

1. Jeremiah uses the four titles for Christ as ways of describing what Jesus will do. Fill in these blanks:
   - as a righteous branch, Jesus will be born in the line of ______
   - as the Lord Our Righteousness, Jesus would __________
   - as a king, Jesus will demonstrate His __________
   - as a shepherd, Jesus will __________
2. Jeremiah twice describes Christ as "righteous." There are two aspects of this. As a priest, Jesus declares us righteous by His ___________ (Ephesians 2:13). As a prophet, Jesus ___________ us both what is right and what God has done to make things right between Himself and us (Mark 6:34). How are these significant?

3. Ephesians 2 speaks of hostility between people and between people and God. Sin is the root of hostility. What kinds of sinful words create walls between people and between us and God? What kinds of actions create walls? What kinds of attitudes do so? See Ephesians 4:25–5:5 and Galatians 5:19–21 for additional examples. How can we aggressively combat these sinful thoughts, words, and actions? See 2 Timothy 3:15–17.

4. What are the three images, or metaphors, which Ephesians 2:19 and 21 use to picture the unity people gain in Christ? What common elements do these images have?

5. Ephesians notes four times that Christ came to make "peace" between us and God and between people. The apostle also said, "Do not repay anyone evil for evil. Be careful to do what is right in the eyes of everybody. If it is possible, as far as it depends on you, live at peace with everyone. … Do not be overcome by evil, but overcome evil with good" (Romans 12:17–18, 21). What can we do to promote peace? How is this similar to the way God treats us? Is it possible to always be at peace with everyone? Why or why not?

Vision

During This Week

1. Think of a situation (past or present) in which you have experienced conflict. Write down ways in which you can promote peace and "overcome evil with good."
2. Is there someone with whom you are in conflict now? Write him or her a "love" note that emphasizes God's love for us in Christ that enables us to love and to forgive one another.

Closing Worship

Read or sing together the stanzas of "Take My Life, O Lord, Renew" (*LW* 404) printed in the Closing Worship activity for session 8.

Scripture Lessons for Next Sunday

Read Exodus 24:3–11, Ephesians 4:1–7, 11–16, and John 6:1–15 in preparation for the next session.

Session 10

Tenth Sunday after Pentecost

Exodus 24:3–11; Ephesians 4:1–7, 11–16; John 6:1–15

Focus

Theme: ***A Heavenly Banquet***

Law/Gospel Focus

Because people are by nature sinful, we are spiritually and emotionally "hungry," and we find little satisfaction. As a result, we are always "restless," hoping something or someone new will provide the companionship and fellowship we want. Jesus Christ invites us to His "feast," which will satisfy by God's grace through faith our hunger for holiness, fellowship with God, and unity with other people. As we receive Christ in the Lord's Supper, He unites us with Him and with one another.

Objectives

By the power of the Holy Spirit working through God's Word we will

1. understand that unity in family and church happens as we gather to hear the Gospel of Jesus Christ proclaimed in worship;
2. recognize that in the Lord's Supper God provides us a foretaste of the heavenly blessings;
3. give thanks for and affirm the diverse gifts God gives to His church to use to serve Him and one another.

Opening Worship

Join together in singing (or saying) the offertory from Divine Service II (*LW*), which speaks of the "bread of life" we receive from Christ and of the "foretaste of the feast to come" which we receive at the Lord's Table (Communion):

> Let the vineyards be fruitful, Lord, and fill to the brim our cup of blessing.

Gather a harvest from the seeds that were sown, that we may be fed with the bread of life.
Gather the hopes and the dreams of all; unite them with the prayers we offer now.
Grace our table with Your presence, and give us a foretaste of the feast to come.

Introduction

It was a quiet supper. Again. Johnny was getting used to it. It seemed that ever since Dad got his promotion at work a few years ago, they hardly saw him anymore. He went to work early and came back late, unless he was out of town.

Mom used to get mad about it, but now she seemed resigned to the long absences. What could they do about it, anyway? The family seemed to be drifting apart.

1. The saying goes, "out of sight, out of mind." When people are apart most of the time, how does this affect their relationships?

2. Traditionally, mealtimes have been times when families could gather and review their days and enjoy time together. Many families find this hard to do with sports, social, school, and work activities all competing for their time. How do these affect family life?

Inform

Scan these summaries of the Scripture lessons for the Tenth Sunday after Pentecost.

Exodus 24:3–11—The Lord establishes a covenant with His people Israel. The blood of the offering seals the covenant. God grants the people forgiveness of sin, and they promise to obey the words of the covenant. The elders feast before God as a sign of their new fellowship. The description of the clear pavement beneath the Lord is similar to that pictured in Revelation 4:6.

Ephesians 4:1–7, 11–16—God's people are united to God through Christ into one body, one faith, and by one Baptism.

John 6:1–15—Jesus Christ provides for His hungry followers. By this, the people recognize that He is the Prophet who was predicted in the Old Testament. Jesus miraculously fed thousands of people on more than one occasion. Jesus demonstrates His compassion for all people—the compassion would eventually take Him to the cross, where He would suffer and die for the sins of all people.

These readings focus on how God provides our needs and unites us with Himself and one another through faith in Christ Jesus.

1. When God established the covenant with his people (Exodus 24), they offered two kinds of sacrifices. Burnt offerings were offered to atone for their sin (Leviticus 1). Fellowship (peace) offerings were offered in thankfulness to God, to fulfill a vow or as a freewill offering. Why was it important for them to begin with a burnt offering? What obstacle to fellowship with God would this remove from the people? When they gave fellowship offerings, what attitudes did this show in the people? How is this progression of events similar to that which occurs in worship?

2. The covenant was based on God atoning for Israel's sin by the blood of the sacrifice. What did the people then pledge to do?

3. What did the elders of Israel do to cement and celebrate their alliance with the Lord (24:11)?

4. Unity among people is built on things they have in common. What seven central things do Christians have in common according to Ephesians 4:6–7?

5. The New Testament uses the "one body" metaphor to picture the unity of Christians. Who is the Head of the body (4:15)? Who are the body parts (4:16)? What kinds of work do we do for each other? What motive must drive all we do (4:16)? What are the two main goals Christ enables us to pursue together (4:13)?

6. Several Old Testament passages speak of God providing food for His people. When Israel was hungry in the wilderness after leaving Egypt, how did God supernaturally feed them (Exodus 16:15)? What parallels are there to Jesus feeding the 5,000? What do these feedings demonstrate about Jesus?

7. The host of a banquet is the one who invites and unites his guests. Who presides over the elders' feast (24:11)? the feast the 5,000 enjoy (6:11)? How does this compare with our celebration of the Lord's Supper in Divine Worship?

8. Ancient prophets had predicted the coming of one who would feed God's people. Isaiah 25:6 and 9 say, "On this mountain the LORD Almighty will prepare a feast of rich food for all peoples, a banquet of aged wine—the best of meats and the finest of wines. … In that day they will say, 'Surely this is our God; we trusted in

Him, and He saved us.' " What did the 5,000 think about Jesus after being miraculously fed by Him (John 6:15)?

Connect

1. One key theme in these passages is that of "feasting with God." Jesus used the image of a banquet to describe heaven:
   Matthew 22:1–14—Invitations to a wedding banquet
   Matthew 25:1–13—10 virgins wait for the bridegroom to arrive at the wedding banquet
   What promises are suggested in these stories? What warnings?

2. Why would Christ choose a banquet as a model for heaven? What is there about a feast that makes it pleasurable? What does this suggest about what heaven will be like?

3. Feasts on earth are partly intended to help us look forward to the "feast to come." Read the words of the offertory "Let the Vineyards" above. What themes do you see here? How do they relate to these passages?

4. What "heavenly meal" do Christians enjoy together during our worship services? In what way is Christ, our Host, present? Note this excerpt from Luther's Small Catechism:

These words, "Given and shed for you for the forgiveness of sins," show us, that in the Sacrament forgiveness of sins, life, and salvation are given us through these words.

What blessings do we receive at this "feast?" How are these a foretaste of heavenly blessings?

5. Christians come from a variety of backgrounds. What does God do with these varied people when they come to His feast (Ephesians 4:3, 13)?

6. In Ephesians St. Paul says that God gave leaders to prepare God's people for service. In the Gospel reading, Jesus tests Philip by asking him what to do for the 5,000. What did Jesus want His disciples to learn from this miracle (John 6:12, 14)?

7. There are many forms of service. Romans 12:4–8 and 1 Corinthians 12:7–11, 27–31 list some of these. You may wish to read these lists to get an idea of the great variety.

Vision

During This Week

Jesus encouraged His disciples to invite to supper not just friends, but poor people who could not "pay them back" by inviting them in return (Luke 14:12–14). Think of someone you know who is poor, away from home, alone, divorced, distraught, disabled, or who for any other reason is not someone you normally invite out socially. Invite them for dinner at your home or at a restaurant.

Closing Worship

Read or sing together the following stanzas of "We Give You But Your Own" (*LW* 405).

We give You but Your own
In any gifts we bring;
All that we have is Yours alone,
A trust from You, our King.

And we believe Your Word,
Though dim our faith, it's true:
What we do for Your people, Lord,
We do it all for You.

Scripture Lessons for Next Sunday

Read Exodus 16:2–15, Ephesians 4:17–24, and John 6:24–35 in preparation for the next session.

Session 11

Eleventh Sunday after Pentecost

Exodus 16:2–15; Ephesians 4:17–24; John 6:24–35

Focus

Theme: *You'll Never Go Hungry*

Law/Gospel Focus

As we face hardship and confusion, we are prone to worry about our future and complain against God for the lot which falls to us. Nonetheless, Christ provides for all of our needs including our greatest need—forgiveness of sin and eternal life. He comes into the "wilderness" of our lives and reveals a plan for us which is greater than our fondest dreams.

Objectives

By the power of the Holy Spirit working through God's Word we will

1. praise and thank God for giving us physical, emotional, and a spiritual life established and grounded in the person and work of Jesus;
2. look to Jesus Christ for spiritual satisfaction, rather than to ourselves or to the tangible things of this world;
3. commit ourselves to Christ and rely on His power to put off sinful ways and put on godly ways.

Opening Worship

Join together in this responsive reading adapted from Psalm 37.

Leader: I was young and now am old,

Participants: Yet I have never seen the righteous forsaken or their children begging bread.

Leader: They are always generous and lend freely;

Participants: Their children will be blessed.

Leader: The Lord will not forsake His faithful ones.
Participants: They will be protected forever.
Leader: Be still and wait patiently for the Lord.
Participants: He is our stronghold in time of trouble.

Introduction

"The bank statement came today," James said over supper. "It seems like there's never enough money for everything."

"We aren't going to lose the house, are we?" Kendra asked her husband.

"No, we made all our bills again this month. We're not behind, but it seems we can never get ahead."

"I'm happy with what we have," Kendra replied.

"I'm not," James retorted. "I guess I'll have to work this Sunday again, although it doesn't seem to help much."

"Then why do it, James? There's more to life than getting ahead. A few more dollars aren't going to make either of us happier."

1. What kinds of complaints did James make? If he did get ahead a little more, do you think he would be happier?

2. There is something James lacks more than money. What is it?

Inform

Scan these summaries of the Scripture lessons for the Eleventh Sunday after Pentecost.

Exodus 16:2–15—Although God miraculously freed Israel from Egypt, the Israelites complained about the food they had to eat. Yet, God graciously provided them manna to eat so that they would know that He is the Lord.

Manna is Hebrew for "What is it?" (16:15). Exodus 16 describes it as thin flakes like frost, white like coriander seed, which tasted like wafers made with honey. It could be ground in mills, beaten in mortars, boiled in pots, and baked into cakes. If left overnight, it became wormy and spoiled, except for the extra portion collected before the Sabbath. This allowed the Israelites to avoid working on the Sabbath by collecting manna on that day. Aaron was told to keep a jar full of manna as a testimony to generations to come.

Ephesians 4:17–24—Christians are commanded to "put off" old, sinful ways, and "put on" a new, godly self through faith in Jesus.

John 6:24–35—Jesus Christ is the true bread from heaven who gives life to the world.

These readings focus on how God provides for all our needs, including our greatest need—forgiveness of sins and eternal life through Jesus Christ.

1. What kind of attitudes did the Israelites have toward Moses and God (Exodus 16:2–3, 7–9)? What did they complain about?

2. What were the people to conclude after seeing manna miraculously appear (Exodus 16:12)?

3. The Israelites were told not to stock up, or hoard, the manna. What do you think some of them did? Why?

4. Why did the Lord give them the simple instructions about not collecting more than a day's worth of manna—except before the Sabbath (Exodus 16:4)? When they obeyed—what spiritual or character traits did this show? What traits did disobedience show?

5. In Ephesians 4:17–19, Paul describes the spiritual nature of the Gentiles. In what ways were they like the Israelites described in Exodus 16?

6. What should Christians "put off?" What should we "put on?"

7. What do people need as the core of their spiritual lives (Ephesians 4:20, John 6:29)? Why?

8. Jesus compares physical bread to Himself, who is the "true bread from heaven" (John 6:32). What two limitations does earthly bread have (John 6:27, 35)? What are three strengths the "bread" Christ gives (John 6:27, 32, 35)?

Connect

1. One key theme in these passages is that of "feasting with God." Jesus often used the image of a banquet to illustrate what life with God after the resurrection will be like. For example, He spoke of the man who invited friends (then strangers) to a banquet, and of the 10 virgins invited to a wedding banquet. What aspects of an earthly banquet apply also to the "heavenly banquet" of life with God?

2. Think about your life as a whole now, and about what you say to others about it. Would an outsider see you as grumbling about much of it? or as joyful? or apathetic? or … what?

3. Make a list of essential "provisions" which our society in general thinks a person must have for a strong and satisfied life. Now make a list of what God considers essential for a strong and satisfied life. How do the lists differ?

4. Jesus said, "Do not work for food that spoils, but for food that endures to eternal life." What would He include under the category "food that spoils?" What would He consider to be "food that endures?" What are some practical ways to "not work for" the one, and to "work" for the other?

5. What "works" does God require (John 6:28–29)? Is this the kind of answer the Jews expected Jesus to give? Why or why not?

6. Read Ephesians 4:19 again. Does this infer that people just "stumble into" trouble, or that people tend to bring many of their problems on themselves? Can you give some examples of this?

7. Ephesians pictures sin as "continual lust for more" (4:19). One can see this inner, unsatiable drive pushing people to more and more sin. How is this true of sins such as pornography, abuse of power, materialism, substance abuse, gambling, and manipulation of people?

8. There are two main steps to rebuilding lives riddled with sin. What are they (Ephesians 4:22)? How can God empower and enable us to begin to do this in concrete ways?

Vision

During This Week

Identify a part of your life that is driven by sinful desires. Confess this sin to God, trusting in the forgiveness Jesus won for you on the cross. Ask that the Holy Spirit would enable and empower you to resist this temptation to sin.

Closing Worship

Speak together Matthew 6:33.

Scripture Lessons for Next Sunday

Read 1 Kings 19:4–8, Ephesians 4:30–5:2, and John 6:41–51 in preparation for the next session.

Session 12

Twelfth Sunday after Pentecost

1 Kings 19:4–8; Ephesians 4:30–5:2; John 6:41–51

Focus

Theme: ***Imitators***

Law/Gospel Focus

When troubles arise, we often feel discouraged, confused, and alone. Christ came to earth to suffer and die for our sinful lack of trust. After He rose from the dead, He promised to be with us always. Jesus' power working in us enables us to face troubles with confidence and hope, and to love those who have hurt us.

Objectives

By the power of the Holy Spirit working through God's Word we will

1. confess to God our frailty of faith when we are faced with obstacles;
2. praise God for sending Jesus to forgive our sinful lack of trust and to provide us encouragement when because of hardships we become discouraged;
3. affirm the power of Christ in our lives that enables us to love even those who hurt us.

Opening Worship

Join in this responsive reading:

Leader: Jesus said, "I am the Bread of life."
Participants: In Him was life, and that life was the light of men.
Leader: Jesus said, "I am the Way and the Truth and the Life,"
Participants: No one comes to the Father except through Him.
Leader: The Spirit says, "Come."
All: Let us take the free gift of the water of life.

Introduction

Police estimate that some 415,000 youth are involved in about 2,500 gangs across the United States. While gangs have long existed in America, the violent nature of gangs has increased. Gang wars commonly erupt over such minor incidents as the theft of a coat or a hint of disrespect, leaving many young people dead. A cycle of revenge occurs as each gang seeks to pay back the other gang for attacks it makes. In this atmosphere, it is not surprising that the life expectancy of core gang members (about 10 percent of the total membership) is only 19.

1. What do you think prompts youth to join gangs?

2. What causes a gang war to continue and expand? What is needed to stop a war once it begins?

3. Can adults also get caught up in a cycle of revenge as they try to pay back their neighbors, (ex-)relatives, or co-workers for their offenses? What ways do people try to pay back others for wrong done? What is needed to stop this chain from continuing?

Inform

Scan these summaries of the Scripture lessons for the Twelfth Sunday after Pentecost.

1 Kings 19:4–8—The prophet Elijah had reached the end of his rope. He felt overwhelmed by enemies, frustration, disappointment, and famine. God responded by strengthening him both physically and

spiritually. A broom tree is a very common desert bush that often grows quite large, so Elijah was able to find some shade under one.

Elijah was involved in a long-term fight against idolatry in Israel. Immediately before this incident, he was part of a miraculous display of God's power over Baal's prophets at Mount Carmel. Yet Ahab's wife Jezebel wanted to kill him.

Ephesians 4:30–5:2—Christians are directed to imitate Christ in their behavior and attitude. In essence, we are called to live a life of unconditional love and forgiveness as Christ did.

John 6:41–51—Those who believe in Jesus Christ have eternal life.

These readings focus on how God provides our needs; especially our greatest need—forgiveness of sin and eternal life.

1. How would you describe Elijah's mood? disinterested? calm? joyful? depressed? apathetic? Is this the kind of reaction one would expect in this type of situation? Why or why not?

2. Elijah was in the desert, though this is the last place one would expect to find food. Who provided food for Elijah? While the food helped him, there was a greater source of strength for him. What was it?

3. Elijah traveled for 40 days. This time period occurs several times in the Bible, including the 40 days of rain on Noah's ark, the 40 days Moses was on Sinai getting the Ten Commandments, and the 40 days Christ was tempted in the desert. In what ways are these situations similar? What meaning may "40" carry in the Bible?

4. We are told not to "grieve" the Holy Spirit. "Grieve" means to bring sorrow, distress, or anguish. Ephesians lists six sins that grieve the Spirit. What are they? Why do these sins in particular grieve the Spirit?

5. Paul exhorts us to have godly attitudes and character. What four key attitudes does he direct us to exercise (4:32, 5:2)? How will these attributes help to strengthen relationships?

6. What one thing did Christ do which shows His love for us more than anything else (5:2)?

7. This section of John 6 is part of a longer section in which Jesus debates the Jews. He repeatedly emphasizes that He is central to a relationship with God and that He is the source (the "bread") of life. The Jews are angry and critical and do not see Him as a source of life. What do they see Jesus as (6:42)? What evidence is there even today that some people see Jesus in this way?

8. Who takes the initiative in people coming to believe in Christ (6:44)? Why does God do this? Which one of God's character traits does this reveal?

Connect

1. The critical question today is the same as it was in Jesus' time—where did Jesus come from? Who really is He? What are the two main answers (John 6:42)? Why are all these answers so important?

2. Jesus Christ used several metaphors to describe Himself, including *life, light, bread,* and *water.* How important are these things to our daily lives? Accordingly, how important is Christ to our spiritual lives?

3. Jesus emphasized how empty, needy, and lost we are without Him in our lives. Without Christ, what kinds of attitudes are bound to reign in a person (Ephesians 4:31)? Without Him, what is our final end (John 6:50)? Without Christ, what are the results of our efforts, work, and conflict with others (1 Kings 19:4)?

4. With Christ in our lives, everything is different. Through faith in Christ, what kinds of attitudes are bound to reign in a person (Ephesians 4:32)? With Him, what is our final end (John 6:47, 51)? With Christ, what are the results of our efforts, work, and conflict with others (1 Kings 19:4)?

5. Christ is essential to our lives. Through faith strengthened by the power of the Holy Spirit working through the means of grace God enables our attitudes and choices to reflect His desires and His love. When we are
   - depressed and frustrated like Elijah, we can ________ Christ to give us __________;
   - bitter or angry at people who hurt us, we can ___________ others as Christ _________ us;
   - confused and don't know what is right, we can __________ to Christ as One who __________ us truth.

6. We are told to "be imitators of God" as children imitate their parents. In particular, we should imitate God's character and attitudes. What is God like (Ephesians 4:32, 5:2)?

Vision

During This Week

Have you, or someone you know, been involved in an ongoing cycle of revenge? What can you do to stop this chain, or to help another person stop it? Confess your desire for vengeance to Jesus, trusting in the forgiveness He won for you on the cross. Then let His love for you shine through you to the person with whom you are in conflict.

Closing Worship

Read or sing stanzas 1–4 of "Oh, Bless the Lord, My Soul" (*LW* 457).

Oh, bless the Lord, my soul!
Let all in me combine
To aid my tongue to bless His name
Whose favor is divine.

Oh, bless the Lord, my soul,
Nor let His mercies lie
Forgotten in unthankfulness
And without praises die.

The Lord forgives my sins,
And He relieves my pain;
The Lord has healed my sicknesses
And made me whole again.

He crowns my life with love,
He ransoms from the grave;
He that redeemed my soul from hell
Has sov'reign pow'r to save.

Scripture Lessons for Next Sunday

Read Proverbs 9:1–6, Ephesians 5:15–20, and John 6:51–58 in preparation for the next session.

Session 13

Thirteenth Sunday after Pentecost

Proverbs 9:1–6; Ephesians 5:15–20; John 6:51–58

Focus

Theme: *Feed on Me*

Law/Gospel Focus

We are surrounded by human ideas and sinful ways of doing things. These influences, along with our own sinful tendencies, often lead us to demonstrate ungodly actions and attitudes. However, God graciously forgives repentant sinners by His grace through faith in Christ Jesus, and by the power of the Holy Spirit working through His Word He empowers us with His wisdom to live godly lives.

Objectives

By the power of the Holy Spirit working through God's Word we will

1. affirm that it is just as important to maintain a healthy spiritual life as it is to maintain a healthy physical life;
2. confess our sinful tendencies and receive the assurance of Christ's forgiveness;
3. give thanks to God for His forgiveness through faith in Christ Jesus and for the wisdom He provides for daily living in His Word;
4. rely on God's Word, not to human opinion, for true wisdom and understanding.

Opening Worship

Join in this responsive reading adapted from Philippians 4:8–9.

Leader: Whatever is true, whatever is noble, whatever is right,

Participants: whatever is pure, whatever is lovely, whatever is admirable—
Leader: if anything is excellent or praiseworthy—
Participants: think on such things.
Leader: Whatever you have learned or received from the Lord—
Participants: Put it into practice.
All: And the God of peace will be with you.

Introduction

"How can you eat that stuff, Tom?" Jackie asked, for probably the hundredth time. "That red meat is going to give you heart disease, the sugar in that dessert is going to make you overweight, the refined flour in that bun is going to make you irregular, and that wine is going to damage your liver!"

"Oh, well," Tom answered, "at least I'll die happy."

"Don't joke about your health," Jackie retorted. "It's too precious to waste. You have to watch what you eat."

1. How much truth is there to Jackie's claim that our diet affects our health?

2. The Bible often uses our everyday activity of eating as an illustration to teach us something about our spiritual lives. How much do the ideas and images we "feed" our minds affect our spiritual lives?

Inform

Scan these summaries of the Scripture lessons for the Thirteenth Sunday after Pentecost.

Proverbs 9:1–6—"Wisdom," which is personified here, is the theme of the whole book of Proverbs. Wisdom is both knowing *and* acting on that which God shares with us in His Word. When people "eat at the table" of wisdom, they receive the assurance of their forgiveness through Christ and the guidance they need to live as the redeemed children of God.

Ephesians 5:15–20—Christians should not live in unwise, sinful ways. Instead, as they are prompted by the Holy Spirit working through God's Word they live their lives reflecting the love of God in Christ Jesus and are able to give thanks to God in all circumstances.

John 6:41–51—Jesus Christ invites us to "eat" of Him, to have faith in Him, and receive through that faith life—abundant life here on earth and eternal life in heaven.

The readings focus on the importance of filling ourselves with God's wisdom provided in His Word. For through God's Word the Holy Spirit works to "make you wise to salvation" and "equip you for every good work."

1. In Proverbs 9:1–6, the Teacher describes a "banquet." What does he offer that is as important and satisfying to our lives as food and wine (verses 1 and 6)?

2. What does a person have to "leave" in order to live by wisdom and understanding (Proverbs 9:6)?

3. Proverbs and Ephesians give specific instructions on how to live wisely. According to Ephesians 5:15–20, what is one foolish thing people should not do (5:18)? What are wise things people do as they are prompted by the Holy Spirit?

4. There are two very different things people can be filled with. What are they (5:18)?

5. Jesus said that people should "eat [His] flesh" and "[drink His] blood" (John 6:54). What do you think Jesus meant?

Clearly, the word *eat* here is a metaphor, or figure of speech. Jesus did not mean that the Jews should pick up knives and forks and become cannibals. When we "eat," we take into our bodies food that is essential for physical life. Jesus is saying that it is just as important to take into our souls the Jesus Christ, because He is essential nourishment for our spiritual lives.

Connect

1. Proverbs uses the word *simple* to mean the opposite of wisdom (not the opposite of "complex," as many people use the word today). "Simple" in Proverbs means "naive, ignorant, and shortsighted." Ephesians mentions one ignorant action—getting drunk. What is there about getting drunk that is attractive to many people? Why is it shortsighted and naive?

2. Drunkenness "leads to debauchery." Why does this happen? Can you recall any times you have seen this happen?

3. Why is being filled with the Spirit so much better than being filled with alcohol (wine)?

4. That which we "feed" or fill our minds affects us. What can result when we fill our minds with
   - pornography

   - Bible passages

   - memories of times people treated us badly

   - television programming that promotes lack of respect or violence

   - consumer advertising

   - Christian hymns and music

5. Sadly, sinful thoughts often fill our minds. As we realize and repent of this, what gift of God can we be especially thankful for?

6. What is the relationship between being filled with the Spirit, speaking psalms to each other, and singing thankful songs to God?

7. What means does the Holy Spirit use to feed our spiritual lives?

8. Although Proverbs 9 speaks of wisdom figuratively, the wisdom of God did become fully realized in the person and work of Jesus. Use 1 Corinthians 1:20–25 to help you describe God's wisdom. What does God's wisdom provide?

Vision

During This Week

Pray daily for someone who feeds of the things of this world. Ask that by your confession of faith the Holy Spirit would work to melt even the most hardened of hearts.

Closing Worship

Read or sing the first stanza of "Let Us Ever Walk with Jesus" (*LW* 381).

Let us ever walk with Jesus,
Follow His example pure,
Through a world that would deceive us
And to sin our spirits lure.
Onward in His footsteps treading,
Pilgrims here, our home above,
Full of faith and hope and love,
Let us do our Father's bidding.
Faithful Lord, with me abide;
I shall follow where You guide.

Scripture Lessons for Next Sunday

Read Joshua 24:1–2, 14–18, Ephesians 5:21–31, and John 6:60–69 in preparation for the next session.

Session 14

Fourteenth Sunday after Pentecost

Joshua 24:1–2, 14–18; Ephesians 5:21–31; John 6:60–69

Focus

Theme: *Whom Will You Serve?*

Law/Gospel Focus

Although we often make promises to be loyal to people and to God, we often fall short of keeping our promises. This unfaithfulness is rooted in our selfish desire to serve ourselves rather than God and our neighbors. God forgives our unfaithfulness through faith in Christ Jesus and calls and empowers us through the Gospel to serve Him, our spouses, our families, and the people of God, just as Christ lived to serve us.

Objectives

By the power of the Holy Spirit working through God's Word we will

1. understand the importance of serving God alone;
2. confess our often self-serving attitudes and actions and receive the assurance of Christ's forgiveness;
3. commit ourselves to love and keep our promises to God, our spouses, and our neighbors as we are empowered by Jesus' total commitment to us as demonstrated by His sacrificial death on the cross.

Opening Worship

Join in this litany adapted from Psalm 128.

Leader: Blessed are those who walk in God's ways,

Participants: May the Lord bless you from Zion.

Leader: Your wife will be fruitful, and your sons like olive shoots,

Participants: May the Lord bless you from Zion.
Leader: May you live to see your children's children.
Participants: Peace be upon us all.

Introduction

"Will you take this woman to be your wife?"

"I do," he said.

"Will you take this man to be your husband?"

"I do," she said.

"Will you be an active member of this church, be faithful in serving others, give sacrificially to the Lord's work, be regular in the use of the Lord's Supper, in worship, and in hearing the Word of God?"

"I will," the new church members said.

"Will you assure that this child we baptize today is brought up in the Christian faith, is taught the Ten Commandments and the Creeds, and is given the Scriptures when this child is able to read, as you continue to pray regularly for his (her) spiritual life and welfare?"

"I will," the godparent replied.

But before much time had passed, "he" and "she" signed a divorce decree, and "they" found other things to do almost every Sunday morning. The godparent had almost forgotten the Baptism, and the child had grown up hardly knowing the God whose love for all people compelled Him to send His only Son to suffer and die on the cross.

We make many promises throughout our lives, but have trouble following through on them. So it is no surprise that nearly half of all marriages fail and a high percentage of church members do little more for their faith than surprising the pastor by their attendance on Christmas Eve and Easter.

1. What major promises have you made in your lifetime? What promises ("little" or "big") have you made in the last few months?

2. Some promises, like marriage vows, dramatically affect our lives. Other promises, like perhaps one to take a son to a ball game "sometime," are less dramatic. But even the "smallest" promises are important. Why? What is at stake even with the "smallest" of promises?

Inform

Scan these summaries of the Scripture lessons for the Fourteenth Sunday after Pentecost.

Joshua 24:1–2, 14–18—Joshua uses the last of his speeches as Israel's leader to challenge the people to commit themselves to serve the true God rather than idols. The Amorites came from a country called Amurru, which was very powerful about the time of Abraham (2000 B.C.). By Moses' time, it had been divided into many independent city-states. In the Old Testament, the word "Amorite" refers to the pre-Israelite population of Palestine in general. Throughout its history, Israel was enticed to follow Amorite gods such as Molech and Ashtoreth rather than the true God.

Ephesians 5:21–31—God calls husbands to love their wives, and wives to submit to their husbands as they together seek to express the unity of being "one flesh" as they serve one another.

John 6:60–69—Jesus Christ challenges His disciples to believe even those of His teachings which are hard for human minds to accept. Peter confesses that Jesus Christ is the Holy One of God who has come into this world to give eternal life.

1. What is the most basic rule of relating to God (Joshua 24:15)? God emphasized its importance by making this the first of the Ten Commandments. What is the First Commandment?

2. What set God apart from the idols of all other nations (Joshua 24:17)?

3. The Lord does not want people to follow Him half-heartedly or to think they can serve the Lord and other gods at the same time.

What challenge does Joshua make to the people (Joshua 24:15)?

4. What motivates Christians to submit to one another (Ephesians 5:21)?

5. Paul compares a Christian's relationship with Christ to a marriage relationship. Which marriage partner does Paul suggest corresponds to Christ? Which is compared to the church?

6. Christ loved and gave Himself up for the church. What does Christ's love motivate husbands to do for their wives? What does Christ's love motivate wives to do for their husbands?

7. Jesus contrasts the Spirit and the ______________________ (John 6:63). What results when people listen to the Spirit? What results when people pay attention to the opposite?

8. The Bible's teaching on predestination had two main aspects. What do the teachings on predestination say about the reason some people are lost (John 6:66)? What does it say about the reason that others have eternal life (John 6:65)? Does John suggest that God induced the disbelievers to turn away from Christ, or that this happened of their own will?

9. We commonly use "Christ" as a title for Jesus of Nazareth. Jesus most often called Himself the "Son of Man." People often misunderstand this title, thinking it refers primarily to His human nature. Read these Bible verses, and write down the things the Son of Man is and does.

   Matthew 12:8

   Matthew 9:6

   Matthew 16:27

   Matthew 26:64

   What do these verses emphasize about Jesus' nature?

Connect

1. Few North Americans today are enticed by idols of the sort the Amorites and some Israelites worshiped. However, other idols compete for worship, attention, devotion, and love from people. People "serve" these idols by investing in them, desiring them, and even sacrificing time, money, and other activities to have them. What "idols" do many people love and serve today?

2. Why did the Israelites find it valuable to serve God instead of idols (Joshua 24:17–18)? Why did Peter want to follow Christ (John 6:68)? What is the greatest thing Jesus did for us (Ephesians 5:25–26)? What other things has God done for us?

3. Peter made a promise to stand by Jesus even if it meant death. Yet as Jesus was standing trial only hours later, Peter denied knowing Him three times. Jesus could have rejected him then as a promise-breaker. What did Jesus choose to do instead (note John 21:15–19)? How does God respond to us when because of sin we deny or reject Him?

4. The Bible speaks of different roles for husband and wife. What primary attitude should a wife have toward her husband (5:22)? Many people today don't even like to say the "S-word" even though it is clearly used here in Ephesians 5. Why does the word *submit* have such a bad connotation to many people today? How might the love of a husband who puts his wife first and would willingly lay down his life for his wife challenge the widely held, negative attitudes toward "submission"? What motivates Christians to sacrifice all to serve Jesus?

5. In response to Jesus' love, husbands love their wives as Ephesians 5:25

   Ephesians 5:28

   Ephesians 5:33

Vision

During This Week

Seek at least one new way to serve your spouse, your children, and/or others you love in response to God's love for you in Christ Jesus—who served you by suffering and dying on the cross for your sins.

Closing Worship

Pray together the Collect of the Day.

O almighty God, whom to know is everlasting life, grant us without all doubt to know Your Son Jesus Christ to be the Way, the Truth, and the Life that, following His steps, we may steadfastly walk in the way that leads to eternal life; through Jesus Christ, our Lord, who lives and reigns with You and the Holy Spirit, one God, now and forever. Amen.

Scripture Lessons for Next Sunday

Read Deuteronomy 4:1–2, 6–8, Ephesians 6:10–20, and Mark 7:1–8, 14–15, 21–23 in preparation for the next session.

Session 15

Fifteenth Sunday after Pentecost

Deuteronomy 4:1–2, 6–8; Ephesians 6:10–20; Mark 7:1–8, 14–15, 21–23

Focus

Theme: *Stand Your Ground!*

Law/Gospel Focus

Because of our sin, we often find ourselves giving in to sin and compromising instead of staying firm in our conviction and obedience to God's Word. God reminds us that His Word is perfect, and it only hurts our lives when we add to, subtract from, or alter it. As God forgives us through faith in Jesus' death on the cross for our sin, He provides us with the faith-strengthening power of the Holy Spirit to defend and to empower us to resist the attack of sin and Satan.

Objectives

By the power of the Holy Spirit working through God's Word we will

1. confess how we have often compromised our faithfulness to God's will for us and our lives and received the assurance of the forgiveness Jesus won for us on the cross;
2. depend on Christ to empower and enable us to follow God's commands;
3. distinguish between God's commands and human traditions;
4. depend on the strength God provides His people by the power of the Holy Spirit working through God's Word.

Opening Worship

Join together in this litany adapted from the Epistle reading for the Fifteenth Sunday after Pentecost.

Leader: Take your stand against the devil's schemes.

Participants: Be strong in the Lord and in His mighty power.

Leader: Our struggle is not against human beings, but against unseen, spiritual forces of evil.

Participants: Be strong in the Lord and in His mighty power.

Leader: Therefore, put on the whole armor of God, so that you can stand your ground when evil comes.

Participants: Be strong in the Lord and in His mighty power.

Introduction

"Jasmine, your Dad and I are concerned that you have moved in with Tom, even though you're not married. That's not what you learned at church or the way you were brought up."

"I know that's not the way things were when you were young," Jasmine answered, "But things are different now. All my friends lived with their boyfriends before they got married. Things change."

"They didn't all marry the boys they lived with, did they?"

"No, Mom. But they didn't all have what Tom and I have. We love each other. That's what's really important, not a license."

1. What do you think is Jasmine's standard for deciding what is right and wrong?

2. What seem to be Jasmine's ideas regarding how firm, long-lasting, and applicable God's Word is?

Inform

Scan these summaries of the Scripture lessons for the Fifteenth Sunday after Pentecost.

Deuteronomy 4:1–2, 6–8—Moses directs Israel to listen carefully and to obey God's laws, because they are righteous. He promises God's blessing to those who follow God's commands.

Ephesians 6:10–20—Paul describes the armor and offensive weapons God gives a Christian for protection against evil powers. The Greek word for "armor" means "all weapons." Some of the armor listed here is mentioned in other parts of the Bible, such as the breastplate and helmet in 1 Thessalonians 5:8. This picture language of fighting against evil powers as one would fight against a foreign army in used in many of Paul's letters.

Mark 7:1–8, 14–15, 21–23—Jesus censured the Pharisees for doing superficial acts of righteousness while their hearts were far from God. The word *hypocrite* is actually a Greek word meaning "actor." When we say "he put on an act," we are using the word in much the same way Jesus did. Jesus concludes this discourse by emphasizing that outward acts do not make a person clean or unclean. Instead, that which comes from a person's sinful heart makes him/her unclean.

These readings focus on how God enables us by the power of the Holy Spirit working through the Word to stand firm against sin and evil powers.

1. Human laws change constantly. God's laws do not change. Because of this, what three things are we instructed to do (Deuteronomy 4:2)?

2. God's people enjoyed two gifts from God which no other nation could claim. What were they (Deuteronomy 4:7–8)?

3. What reward did God's people receive when they followed God's law (4:1)?

4. What enemies do Christians face (Ephesians 6:11–12)?

5. Paul uses the illustration of a soldier's armor to describe several spiritual characteristics God provides to protect us from evil. What six elements does he list (Ephesians 6:14–17)? Which of these is the offensive weapon?

6. The Jews carried out many religious practices such as cleanliness laws as they sought to obey God's commands. However, they had two serious problems. What were they (Mark 7:6–8)?

7. Temptations such as money, sex outside of marriage, and fighting, have no influence over us in themselves. What is the real source of temptation to sin (Mark 7:21)?

8. Does Jesus describe sin as something outside of us, or as something that comes from within us? What is the significance of this?

Connect

1. God uses the means of grace—Word and Sacrament—to strengthen our faith. What means and schemes does the devil use to hinder faith or to draw us to sin?

2. One person may be tempted by something, such as money, while another person is not. Why the difference? What kinds of things are the most powerful temptations in your life?

3. The "sword of the Spirit" is the Word of God. How did Jesus wield the sword in His battles against temptation (Matthew 4, Luke 4)? How can we fix God's Word strongly in our minds so that we are able to use it against the enemy?

4. Jesus quotes Isaiah, condemning those whose "hearts are far from Me." The opposite is to keep our hearts close to Him. How can a Christian go about doing this?

Vision

During This Week

Plan to have additional opportunities to put on the full armor of God—devotions, Bible study, prayer, worship. Set aside time for these activities daily. Pray that through these opportunities the Holy Spirit would empower you to resist temptation.

Closing Worship

Read or sing together the stanzas 1 and 4 of "A Mighty Fortress is Our God" (*LW* 297).

A mighty fortress is our God,
A sword and shield victorious;
He breaks the cruel oppressor's rod
And wins salvation glorious.
The old satanic foe
Has sworn to work us woe.
With craft and dreadful might
He arms himself to fight.
On earth he has no equal.

God's Word forever shall abide,
No thanks to foes, who fear it;
For God Himself fights by our side
With weapons of the Spirit.
Were they to take our house,
Goods, honor, child, or spouse,
Though life be wrenched away,
They cannot win the day.
The Kingdom's ours forever.

Scripture Lessons for Next Sunday

Read Isaiah 35:4–7a, James 1:17–22 (23–25), 26–27, and Mark 7:31–37 in preparation for the next session.